BREATHE DEEPLY

My Journey Through Hyperbaric Oxygen Therapy

by

Greg Hadley

Title ID: 8062385

ISBN 10: 1-9843-5263-6
ISBN 13: 978-1984352637

Printed in the United States of America

Hadley, Greg [1934 --]
  Breathe Deeply: My Journey Through Hyperbaric
  Oxygen Therapy (First Edition)

Other Books by Greg Hadley

God Only Knows!
What Happens When We Die

Mercy Remembered
(co-author Rev. Richard Berg CSC)
Commemorating the Jubilee Year of Mercy

Life is Good
Reflections on a Fulfilled Human Journey – a Memoir

Spiritual G. P. S.
A Roadmap for Your Salvation Journey

Jesus Face to Face
Tales of Fleeting Personal Encounters with The Christ found in the New Testament Gospels

Twilight Reflections
Where the Elderly Find God

Aging: The Autumn Phase of Life
How to Navigate Through the Golden Years

God's Words to My Heart

100 Everyday Epiphanies
Simple Events That Can Inspire Prayer

Common Problems; Common Sense Solutions
A Primer for Small Business Owners

Fundamentals of Baseball Umpiring [1]

---

[1] *In the National Baseball Hall of Fame, Cooperstown, NY*

Table of Contents

PREFACE 1

WHAT IS HYPERBARIC OXYGEN THERAPY? 3

HOW DID I COME TO THIS THERAPY? 11

PERSONAL REFLECTIONS ON HYPERBARIC OXYGEN THERAPY 17

THE INITIAL VISIT 19

THE TECHNOLOGY 21

OTHERS BEING TREATED...23

THE CLINIC STAFF 25

PALPABLE FEAR 27

DISAPPOINTMENT 29

DISTRESS 31

TRANSPORTATION ANGELS 33

TIME MANAGEMENT 35

PAIN OR DISCOMFORT?..37

A SETBACK...39

FATIGUE 41

UNCERTAINITY OF THE OUTCOME 43

"NEWBIES" 45

THE NECESSITY OF HOPE 47

THE HOOD..49

GRATITUDE 51

MINDFULNESS AND MEDITATION 53

PATIENCE 55

SUPPORT GROUPS 57

THE LAST DAY..59

EPILOGUE 61

Reference Material

Reference materials produced by Legacy Health Systems:

- *"Healing Through Hyperbaric Treatment,"* a brochure.

- *"What You Need to Know About Hyperbaric Treatment,"* a fact sheet.

- "Hyperbaric Medicine Clinic," a fact sheet.

- *"Remember!"* a fact sheet.

- *"Hyperbaric Oxygen Therapy,"* a fact sheet.

Numerous Internet web sites were examined that offered information on such topics as hyperbaric oxygen therapy, the causes and manifestations of radiation cystitis, treatment protocols for radiation cystitis, prescribed uses of radiation beam therapy, post prostate surgery treatment and other related subjects. Especially noted is the Undersea and National Board of Diving and Hyperbaric Medical Technology (www.nbdhmt.org).

PREFACE

This little booklet was written while I was undergoing forty Hyperbaric Oxygen Therapy (HBOT) treatments. Because most people are not familiar with this type of medical therapy, I felt the impressions and feelings of a lay person who had experienced these treatments first hand might be helpful to those who would follow me. Obviously, I lack the medical training to fully explain how this protocol works with precise detail. However, I can tell you about the program from my perspective and what led me to try this course of treatment. My explanation will include information about the medical condition I am hoping to mitigate and some additional ailments of others that are apparent candidates for this method of medical therapy.

Beyond just a series of medical treatments, I found the experience to be profoundly spiritual. The long daily sessions in a completely enclosed space allowed me to think deeply about what might be happening to my soul as well as my body. So, I have concluded this little booklet with a series of reflections that might touch others in the deepest part of their being. That is my hope. Please let me know what you think about this small work after you have read it.

Contact me at: greghadley34@msn.com

WHAT IS HYPERBARIC OXYGEN THERAPY?

When my doctor first mentioned Hyperbaric Oxygen Therapy (HBOT), I had no idea what he was talking about. I dimly recalled some type of hyperbaric tank used during World War II to treat deep sea divers or submariners who rose too quickly from deep under the sea to the surface that caused lung and blood disorders. These people were immediately put into a tube containing high levels of oxygen. This treatment apparently worked to cleanse their lungs and blood from the toxic gases that developed during their rapid ascent. The exact nature of their medical difficulties or how the treatment worked to relieve them was a mystery to me.

Now I have completed a rigorous course of forty Hyperbaric Oxygen Therapy treatments (HBOT) at the clinic located at Legacy Emanuel Hospital in Portland, Oregon. While I understand why my medical advisors suggested this therapy and what the hoped-for outcome will be, I can't tell you I clearly understand *exactly* how this treatment works to achieve healing. So, this little booklet may provide you with some of the "what" of hyperbaric oxygen therapy, but not offer the "how" that you are seeking. That answer may only be available to Medical Doctors with special training and Board Certification in this medical specialty.

From a layman's perspective, I know that patients with some of the following health problems may benefit from HBOT:

- Diabetic ulcers of the lower extremities.
- Acute peripheral arterial insufficiency.
- Compromised skin grafts.
- Tissue damage caused by radiation therapy.
- Gas embolisms and gas gangrene.
- Crush injuries and severed limbs.
- Carbon monoxide and cyanide poisoning.

This is just a short list. Many other conditions with difficult to pronounce medical names may be candidates for HBOT as well.

Every patient is checked daily before entering the hyperbaric chamber for treatment. Blood pressure and temperature are taken. Current levels of pain are determined. Technicians ask questions about cold symptoms, changes in medications or any issues the patient may be experiencing. For those with diabetes, blood sugar levels are carefully monitored. No one can enter the hyperbaric chamber without receiving this vital sign checkup.

How does HBOT work? Patients (up to a maximum of eight people) enter a tubular metal chamber that is approximately 8' in diameter and 25' long. On each side of the chamber are padded benches for seating those undergoing treatment. Above the seating areas there is an array of valves and controls required to handle the gases involved in the therapy. When there are only a few people for a session, some may actually have room to lie down. In addition to the patients, there is a staff technician present in the tube. Another staff member is outside the tube at a command center, controlling the process going on inside the chamber.

When everyone is inside, a large steel door on one end is closed and pressurization begins. During the next ten minutes, pressurization is applied until the inside of the chamber is at an equivalent depth of 40' under water. While this is happening, the inside of the tube becomes quite warm, perhaps as high as 90^0 Fahrenheit. Patients and staff also feel the increasing pressure in their ears. It is important to equalize pressure in the ears by swallowing, yawning and other techniques. Failure to do this may result in damage to the ear drums. Once pressure levels are reached, ear popping or crackling subsides.

The time it takes to reach the desired level of pressurization is called "The Dive." Once this phase is complete, each patient is fitted with a large clear plastic hood covering the head. The hood is roughly the shape of an elongated hat box. The hood is connected to a snug fitting collar worn by each patient. On the underside of the collar are two fittings that connect to flexible plastic tubing. One tube is attached to 100% oxygen; the other tube exhausts carbon dioxide. Because the oxygen is being delivered under high pressure, the patients are able to breathe 10.5 times the amount of oxygen they normally would. In routine daily activities, we only breathe about 21% oxygen.

Once depth is reached and helmets are in place, the therapeutic session begins. For the next ninety minutes, the patient will breathe the highly concentrated oxygen. The session is divided into three thirty-minute periods, the first two sessions followed by a five-minute break with the hood off. At the end of the third thirty-minute period, the chamber is de-pressurized and brought back to sea level. During this phase, the chamber becomes quite cold and, at the very end, a light mist may form. Once again, patients will feel slight ear pressure, but nothing like on a dive. In summary, each routine session is 117 minutes in length, ten minutes to achieve pressurization, 100 minutes of therapy and seven minutes to de-pressurize.

The $64,000 question: How does this work to heal wounds and restore damaged cells? According to Enoch Huang, M.D., medical director for the hyperbaric medicine center at Legacy Emanuel, "Oxygen under pressure acts like a drug when it dissolves into the blood. This helps speed cell repair and form new blood vessels, which in turn assists in the healing of wounds." Dr. Huang continues: "Repeated exposure to pressurized oxygen give a lifeline to ischemic (compromised blood flow) tissue, boosts the effects of some antibiotics, activates white blood cells to fight certain infections, reduces tissue swelling, and promotes the healing process of specific chronic wounds."

The preceding paragraph represents my understanding of this medical healing procedure. As you will read later, I entered this treatment process hoping for relief or improvement from a medical condition known as radiation cystitis. I have a lot of compromised or damaged tissue in many of my pelvic organs due to radiation therapy I received after prostate cancer surgery 16 years ago.

Before entering the hyperbaric chamber, each patient must change out of street clothes down to their underwear. Blue scrub tops and pants are provided along with paper foot "booties." The clinic also provides changing rooms and lockers for those going through treatment.

Those receiving Hyperbaric Oxygen Therapy must comply with an extensive list of safety regulations and staff enforces these rules rigorously. There is a long list of prohibited items that cannot be taken into the chamber. Patients are advised not to wear or bring into the chamber the following: makeup, perfume, aftershave, hairspray, hair oils, gels, wigs, hairpieces, extensions, nail polish, alcohol, petroleum-based products, jewelry, hearing aids, or electronic devices of any kind. This is just a partial list. The general rule about prohibited articles can be summed up as follows: "If you weren't born with it or we didn't give it to you, you probably can't take that article into the chamber with you." Eye glasses are an exception to this rule.

Why is all this emphasis on safety so important? Many will remember the incident in 1967 when three of our original NASA astronauts— "Gus" Grissom, Ed White and Roger Chaffee—were killed in a static test of an Apollo space capsule. It was determined that an electrical spark ignited a fire which spread rapidly, due in part, to a 100% oxygen environment within the capsule. That grizzly accident surely helped to form safety protocols for any confined spaces with a 100% oxygen environment like a hyperbaric chamber. While any danger is greatly mitigated by current technology, it is important to recognize that a highly concentrated oxygen environment poses safety concerns.

How is success measured for HBOT? There are a very wide variety of ailments that can be effectively treated with this therapy. The percentage of cure or improvement will vary greatly depending on the condition being treated. In my particular case—damaged tissue due to radiation therapy—I was told that there was a 70% chance I would achieve significant improvement with my condition. At no time was "cure" ever mentioned to me. Obviously, the terms "significant improvement" and "a 70% chance..." are somewhat nebulous and do not come with a clear metric for measurement. However, I view a 70% chance of an improved situation to be worth the effort required to complete a normal course of HBOT treatments.

Each patient in HBOT therapy has a meeting with the clinic doctor about every two weeks. During this session, the doctor reviews how the patient is tolerating the therapy, focusing on potential problems with ear drums and eyesight that may be affected. Of course, the doctor also tries to determine how each patient is healing and whether or not progress is being made. Finally, the doctor will answer any of the patient's questions and make an assessment about the number of future sessions that may be required to achieve the desired goal.

Is there any downside to Hyperbaric Oxygen Therapy? There are some risks, for sure. During "The Dive" it is important to equalize the pressure in your ears. Failure to do that could result in serious injury to your ear drums. Some may experience claustrophobia (medical personnel prefer to call this "space confinement anxiety") when entering the chamber. On a personal note, I have a strong claustrophobia syndrome but have not been adversely affected when entering the comparatively spacious hyperbaric chamber. Some will experience a diminution of eyesight. The oxygen under pressure can somewhat distort the shape of the eyeball during a normal course of therapy. I am advised that eyesight will return to prior levels within 6-8 weeks after the conclusion of therapy.

I think the biggest problem one faces is the utter boredom of each two-hour therapy session. One can read a book, but the lighting is just fair, and the plastic hood creates some visual distortion. Streaming videos or DVDs are available, but it is difficult to satisfy the tastes of all the people in the chamber. In addition, some of the action-oriented videos are quite loud and can annoy those who may be nodding off or reading. So, it turns out to be a long two-hour stint. Add to that the arrival time at least one-half hour before the beginning of therapy, getting to and from the clinic and changing of clothes before and after each session. This all adds up to a large chunk of time plucked out a daily schedule.

I have experienced that HBOT healing is often not linear. Some wounds being healed will actually get worse before they get better. I have found this to be true and others have told me they have had similar results. It can be discouraging to observe apparent progress only to experience a setback further into therapy. I was advised of this situation before I began the sessions; it helped when it happened to me.

Hyperbaric Oxygen Therapy is probably not a magic bullet for all wounds. It does seem to have the potential to alleviate many conditions and provide users with an enhanced quality of life. If that winds up being the end result of my own course of HBOT, I will consider it to be a worthwhile medical intervention for me.

HOW DID I COME TO THIS THERAPY?

I had scheduled an October 2017 appointment with Dr. Michael Gardner, a urologist. Dr. Gardner has managed my post-prostate cancer surgery care for a number of years. I trust his medical advice. I was in his office to discuss my on-going treatment for a condition called radiation cystitis. This is a complication of radiation therapy to pelvic tumors such as prostate cancer. High intensity beam radiation, sometime required after prostate cancer surgery can cause extensive damage to the cells of the bladder and other pelvic organs. The obvious manifestation of this problem is hematuria, or blood in the urine.

Dr. Gardner's principal recommendation was that I begin Hyperbaric Oxygen Therapy. He felt that this offered the best chance to reverse the negative effects of radiation cystitis. He commented that additional surgical intervention probably did not offer a positive outcome for me. Dr. Gardner handed me some written material on the treatment. He made no attempt to portray himself as an expert with this therapy but had been convinced by Dr. Enoch Huang that this approach could be very helpful to patients dealing with various forms of radiation cystitis. Gardner suggested I contact Dr. Huang and schedule an appointment to obtain additional details and get my questions answered.

Elsewhere in this document, I have done my best to explain, in laymen's terms, what Hyperbaric Oxygen Therapy is, how it works, what are its risks and potential rewards.

I was diagnosed with prostate cancer early in 2002. My father had died of the disease in 1965. Because it was potentially familial in nature, I had been very faithful with appropriate testing to determine my status. During my 2002 physical, my PSA (Prostate Specific Antigen) blood test surged beyond normal levels, so I sought the advice of a local, well recommended urologist/surgeon about my condition. In a few short weeks, my PSA continued to rise so a biopsy was conducted. The results of that procedure clearly indicated that I had a fast growing, aggressive cancer. There was concern that the tumor might have already escaped the prostate capsule. If true, this could lead to a very serious outcome.

In July 2002, I underwent a radical prostatectomy, i.e., a complete surgical removal of the prostate gland. Statistically, many men who undergo a radical prostatectomy are completely cured by the operation although some may experience undesirable side effects after the cancer is successfully removed. While I was convinced that the surgeons had done their best, post-operative testing showed that some cancer had escaped the capsule leaving dangerous cells lurking in my pelvic bed waiting to metastasize to my bones or other organs.

My medical advisors recommended that I enter a course of radiation therapy. Usually, this involves 30-40 episodes of focused beam radiation aimed at the pelvic bed. The treatments themselves are non-invasive and painless but I was advised to expect increasing levels of fatigue as the therapy was administered even continuing after the treatments were completed. I was also told that I might experience appetite loss and other negative side effects. I do not recall that anyone discussed the potential for long term side effects from the therapy.

I began my radiation treatments in December 2002 and they continued through January 2003. As advised, I found myself sluggish and fatigued during the therapy and for several weeks thereafter. I was also dogged by the most common side effects of prostate surgery and several medical interventions provided little to no relief. Otherwise, I tried hard to maintain a regular exercise routine and by late spring 2003 all indications were that the radiation had been effective. Routine PSA testing consistently resulted in an "undetectable" reading meaning that there was no active cancer activity related to the cells that escaped from my prostate.

While all of this was good news, my doctors cautioned that I should consider my cancer "in remission" but not necessarily cured since some remaining tumor cells may have survived the radiation. But, with continuing negative PSA readings and a return to general good health, I was able to resume my previously active life style. I felt well, was able to deal with the negative consequences of prostate surgery side effects and returned to life as it had been.

The way I looked at it, the radiation treatments had probably saved my life—certainly they extended it—and I was fortunate indeed. I felt that there might be something I was called to do with the rest of my life. I had absolutely no idea what that was, but I did feel blessed and grateful to Almighty God for the additional time he had given to me.

A couple of years later, I experienced a small amount of blood in my urine. There was no pain associated with this incident, but I was startled and immediately called my primary care physician seeking his advice. (The urologist who had performed my surgery had left his practice, was now teaching at a local medical school and I had not, as yet, engaged a new urologist). My doctor did not seem overly concerned about the hematuria. He told me to be observant and let him know if it happened again. He pointed out that radiation can damage cells in the pelvic organs and that some of this bleeding could merely represent sloughing off scar tissue.

Now it is 2018. I am close to 84 years of age. The symptoms described have become progressively worse and more frequent. Following medical advice, I have just completed forty sessions of HBOT. At the outset, I was given good odds that "significant" improvement could be expected. I am unsure exactly what metrics measure my success. Intuitively, I feel there has been some improvement although not as much as I hoped for. Perhaps there may be a carry-forward effect that will result in further gains in the future. I hope that is true; time will tell.

I suppose this is an unfinished story. I wanted to make this booklet coincide with the end of my treatment. At this point, I hope all readers will join me in hoping for a happy ending.

Breathe Deeply

PERSONAL REFLECTIONS ON HYPERBARIC OXYGEN THERAPY

When I told my Pastor, Father Richard Berg CSC, that I was going to commence a course of Hyperbaric Oxygen Therapy, he was immediately upbeat about my prospects. First, he was pleased that I was doing something positive to alleviate the nagging medical condition that was sucking my energy and making daily life a negative experience. When I explained the treatment to Father Dick, his face lit up with a big smile and he said, "You're a very lucky man!" I was puzzled. I told Father that each individual session was long and boring and that I had to do this at least forty times. I asked, "Why do you think I'm lucky, Father?" He responded, "Well, if you plan each session correctly, you will have the opportunity to make a forty-day spiritual retreat. Most of us don't have time for such a thing in our busy daily schedules. But you will, and that's why I refer to you as lucky."

Father Berg was suggesting that I approach each therapy session like it was a mini-retreat. A time for reflection, a time to find meaning in the ordinary events of the therapy, a time to come face-to-face with the Divine Creator, the Great Physician, the Almighty Spirit. If I was able to focus and appreciate the time set aside for the daily therapy, I might not only enhance my physical life but my spiritual life as well. A great idea, I thought! Father Berg added, "Not only that, but record your thoughts and feelings in a small booklet you can share with others, especially those who have gone through the same treatment series or may be faced with it in the future."

The following chapters are a series of my reflections. I hope you enjoy them.

THE INITIAL VISIT

The hyperbaric clinic is located in a large hospital complex. Being unfamiliar with the location, I went to the main entrance figuring they would direct me. In reality, I was quite a distance from the clinic. After several phone calls, a hospital aide arrived, put me into a wheel chair and pushed me through a labyrinth of underground corridors to the clinic reception area. Soon after arriving, I was escorted to a treatment room. A young nurse asked me a series of medical questions and took my blood pressure. The numbers were very high; the stress about being in the wrong place and my apprehension about what I was getting into drove the numbers up.

I was joined by Dr. Enoch Huang, the clinic director. He was an amiable young man, probably in his mid-thirties, exuding confidence and competence. Speaking in a friendly, even-paced tone he explained how the therapy worked, what I could expect and the risks I was accepting. I asked several questions which he directly answered without equivocation. In less than ten minutes, I had been told I would probably need forty therapy sessions, there was a 70% chance I would experience significant improvement and that I should start treatment in one week.

No one re-took my blood pressure. I'm sure it would have still been high. Frankly, I had serious misgivings about this whole adventure. I guess you could say that I was scared.

Have you ever been scared? Health, financial, family or career concerns can leave anyone feeling distressed, worried or afraid. What is the antidote? Trust in God. "I will never send you more than you can handle," he has told us. But, trust is really hard, isn't it?

Father God, please send me the grace to trust in you.

THE TECHNOLOGY

Today was my first day. Five of us were scheduled for the 1:00 PM "dive." First, we strip to underwear in changing rooms and don scrubs. All undergo a test of vital signs—blood pressure, temperature and an eye exam (treatments will temporarily affect eyesight negatively). Two of us "newbies" have the collar that holds our head piece fitted tightly to our neck. All is ready; we take the few steps from the waiting room to the hyperbaric chamber and take our seats. A tech is with us. The chamber is about eight feet in diameter and twenty-five feet long. Padded benches accommodating eight people line the sides. Above each bench are control valves, plastic tubes, nozzles and other equipment. On the far wall is a television screen to show movies.

Initial pressurization seals and locks the large round door in place. The chamber is then pressurized equal to a forty-foot depth under water. Swallowing, yawning and jaw movement helps to unblock ears under pressure. Now begins the two-hour session with a plastic helmet attached to our neck collars. Other than slight "popping" of the ears and changes in temperatures while pressurizing and depressurizing there is no discomfort. Two hours pass very slowly. Maximum patience is needed.

What kinds of minds devise this equipment and their medical treatment protocols? Only a few years ago, such devices were non-existent. Yet today, five souls are being treated for various ailments because of the ingenuity and creativity of someone seeking a solution to a medical problem that was previously unsolvable.

Great Physician, we humbly thank you for those engineers, medical personnel and entrepreneurs who develop new approaches to improving the span of life you have gifted to each one of us.

OTHERS BEING TREATED

Initially, four people shared my treatment regime. Brenda, a fifty-something with pink hair, has two more sessions to go. She's a little loud but friendly to all. Lina is a young lady, quiet, reserved and a student, I think. Will is a fifty-something, trim, good looking, and casually outgoing. He has completed fifteen sessions. Sydney is a quiet military veteran, maybe late 70's with little to say. Syd started his treatments with me.

Everyone is cordial, courteous but not forthcoming. The "veterans" provide tips to newcomers and "show us the ropes." We share the same medical treatment but little personal information about ourselves and nothing about our deepest feelings. This is to be expected. Our relationship is superficial, bound together only by the hope that this daily two-hour treatment will make life better, less difficult and possibly longer. What we feel in the deepest part of our beings can only be shared with those with whom we are more viscerally connected. We five are merely travelers on a train headed to a common destination. Nothing else ties us together.

Too much of today's social interaction resembles the five of us sharing a hyperbaric tube. People are engrossed in high tech devices, ignoring those walking beside them. Texting, email, SnapChat, and Facebook let us communicate to everyone and talk to no one. Many are constantly in touch yet experience deep loneliness. This can't be good. How do we promote the feeling that we are all in this together?

ﻙﻙﻙ

God, the great Communicator, please instill in each of us the ability and willingness to be in touch with our neighbors in a meaningful way.

THE CLINIC STAFF

Every day we encounter four people at the clinic. Maria is the receptionist, mans the phones and schedules appointments. Charlotte is the team leader and helps prepare us for our daily treatments. Ken is a young technician who is often assigned as the staff member inside the tube during treatments. James is a little older and rotates as the one who operates the control panel outside the tube regarding pressure, timing and other technical requirements. After a while, I assume the work is very routine and probably boring. Yet, each step of the daily treatment seems carefully planned and executed. Staff must go through this twice each day— morning and afternoon. I'm sure there are other duties they perform but they are hidden from those being treated.

We casually show up for medical treatments that are highly technical and complex employing sophisticated equipment. Most of us give little thought to all the technicians needed to assist in our treatments. What motivated them to choose this vocation? What training have they received? Do they find their work to be meaningful and fulfilling? Does their employment provide an adequate level of financial security and opportunities for professional growth? Those of us benefitting from their labor probably will never know the answers to most of those questions.

ひひひ

Lord, we thank you for all those who assist in our healing process. Even though we may not express our thanks, let them know how much we appreciate and are grateful for the work they perform each day.

PALPABLE FEAR

Today there were visitors to the clinic. A late forty-ish mother accompanied her twenty-something daughter for a tour of the facilities. The young woman apparently had been scheduled for a series of hyperbaric oxygen treatments. She and her mother were being introduced to the program and how things worked. The older woman seemed interested and inquisitive while her daughter was literally trembling with nervousness. The staff conducting the tour was making a special effort to soothe the young lady's apprehension—with little success.

After the visitors returned from touring the chamber itself, they passed the waiting room where four of us waited in our blue scrubs to begin today's treatment. The anxious young woman asked no one in particular, "How is it in there? How do you feel?" I spoke up with a confident smile and replied, "It's OK, don't worry. You're not the first person who has had this treatment and you won't be the last. Believe me, it will be fine, and you'll do great." The young woman visibly shed her concern and said, "That is so reassuring! Thanks for telling me that." Mom and daughter left the clinic with big smiles on their faces.

I didn't tell the young lady anything that wasn't true. Sure, I could have said the treatments were not much fun, could be very boring and removed a big chunk of time out of your schedule. But, she needed reassurance not something negative. She will learn about the less positive aspects of this treatment soon enough.

ৼৼৼ

Lord, when you provide an opportunity, please give me the grace to be positive, uplifting and encouraging to others. Everyone is entitled to a gentle arm around the shoulder or pat on the back when they are facing uncertainty and glimpsing into the unknown.

DISAPPOINTMENT

After each ten days, those in treatment have a face-to-face meeting with Dr. Huang, the clinic director. The purpose of this appointment is to gauge how we are tolerating the daily treatments and, more importantly, if we are experiencing any improvement in our condition. Yesterday one of my current "mates" met with the doctor. Initially, the patient had been advised that he should plan on thirty treatments. It was expected that this would provide a significant reduction in symptoms, if not a cure. When I first met this man, he had completed his fifteenth treatment and was happy to be more than half way done. Something is yesterday's meeting caused the doctor to move the goal line for him. Now, instead of thirty treatments, Dr. Huang was suggesting that forty treatments were necessary. The patient was visibly disappointed with this news. While maintaining a stoic, upbeat manner, he wasn't pleased with this turn of events.

Throughout our lives, events occur that force us to modify our plans resulting in regret and disappointment. Maturity is sometimes defined as neither getting too euphoric when things go well nor being too depressed when things go badly. Easy to say, but not always easy to do. Our ability to display equanimity in the face of disappointment may be aided by the words from a common prayer, "...Thy will be done on earth as it is in heaven."

જીજીજી

Father God, we try to maintain an optimistic attitude especially when we are engaged in a treatment therapy like hyperbaric oxygen. Each day brings the possibility of a disappointing outcome. Help us to forge ahead even in the face of difficulties and unsatisfactory results.

DISTRESS

All of us were ready to enter the hyperbaric tube for our daily treatment. Suddenly there was a flurry of activity as two staff members exited the chamber with a patient on a gurney. Although we were not told anything, it was apparent that this patient had been receiving some type of solitary hyperbaric treatment and was now on her way back to someplace in the hospital. It was also easy to discern that this patient was suffering profound discomfort, probably intense levels of pain. She was emitting high pitched moans and groans as she lay strapped on the gurney awaiting transportation. Each of us in the waiting room felt empathy with the patient although none of us was capable of alleviating her agony.

All four of us were bearing a health burden that led us to this form of treatment. While our individual conditions were more or less serious, we all decided that none of our problems matched the severity of that lonely patient on the gurney. It was agreed between us that if everyone in the world could gather and throw all of their problems into a common pile, each person would probably be happy to take back that which they had contributed to that heap of misery. No matter how difficult our own problems were, someone else certainly faced even greater difficulties.

When faced with tough medical treatment choices, it is easy to say, "Woe is me!" We wonder what karma has led to this need for arduous and inconvenient treatment. That is, until we observe someone in worse shape than we are in.

❧❧❧

Lord, help me to keep things in context when I am facing tough challenges in my own life. Guide me to recognize that others suffer, too.

TRANSPORTATION ANGELS

One of the major inconveniences involved with this hyperbaric treatment is location. The only therapy equipment in the Portland Metro area is almost 16 miles from my home. The trip involves two high use freeways and crossing a bridge. On the way home, the trip is into the teeth of the rush hour traffic that is congested and slow. Thankfully, my retirement community provides medical transportation for the residents. Each day I am picked up at 11:45 AM and delivered to the treatment center. At approximately 3:15 PM a car and driver arrives to pick me up and take me home. Those guys who drive me to and from each day are angels. I don't think I would make it without their help. Roger, the supervisor, Thomas, Tom, Richard, Bart, Joe and Allen each have pick-up duties. All of them are conscientious, careful drivers and treat their resident passengers with the utmost helpfulness and courtesy. Of course, some of the men become favorites but each one is highly valued and save us from the onerous task of driving our own cars to medical appointments. Thanks to all you guys!

Stop and think about your life. Most of us couldn't get through a routine day without the assistance of many people. Newspaper delivery people; restaurant waiters; bus drivers; retail clerks; doctors and nurses; police and fire personnel—the list of those helping us through most days is almost endless. Do you believe that most of us are duly appreciative to those who help us get through the day? No, I don't either.

✌✌✌

Lord, you had Simon of Cyrene help you on your way to Calvary. Help me accept and appreciate all the Simons in my life.

TIME MANAGEMENT

Hyperbaric oxygen treatment takes a huge chunk of time. I soon found that I would have to reorganize my life to complete basic chores. Each day I leave my home at 11:45 AM and it is about 4:30 PM when I return. Important things still needed to be done. When do I exercise? I try to attend daily Mass—will that be possible? How about getting a haircut? I need to see other doctors; when can I schedule them? How about my afternoon "power nap;" can I fit that in? I still have consulting clients and keep in touch with numerous colleagues via email; how can I complete that? Our car needs service occasionally—when? Approximately twenty-five hours a week has been carved out of my personal life. Every human being is identical in one particular—we each have 24 hours per day available to us, not one second more or less. I had to learn what is crucial and what can be put off, eliminated or laid off on others.

Many of us could use some scrutiny of our time management. Seconds, minutes, even hours slip through our fingers, time which may be devoted to more productive enterprise. Idleness is not all bad; time set aside for meditation, prayer or passive rest may actually be beneficial. A review of our schedules may also show that we often squander time that could be used more purposefully. Have you thought about your own time management lately?

✍✍✍

> *Dear Lord, help me to understand what a precious gift time is to me. When I use the time allotted to me poorly, I have no chance of ever making it up As the Jesuit Fathers preach, "Everything we do should be for God's greater honor." Show me how to use my time that way.*

PAIN OR DISCOMFORT?

I am asked: Does the hyperbaric therapy involve any discomfort? Initially there are lots of plugged ears as the chamber is pressurized. Yawning, jaw movement and holding one's nose while blowing all help to alleviate the congestion. Failure to clear this ear pressure could result in a ruptured ear drum. While the pressurization is taking place, the chamber becomes very warm. No pain but a little uncomfortable.

Once we reach the desired pressure—equivalent to 40' under water—the temperature reverts to a comfortable level. Then large clear plastic hoods are placed over our heads and secured to the rings around our necks. This may cause space confinement anxiety for some. Biggest problem is the inability to fix a runny nose or itchy face. Hoods are in place for ninety minutes with two five-minute breaks when they are removed. You can see through the hoods to read a book or watch a movie but there are some visual distortions in the plastic that are annoying. With the hoods in place, one hears a constant "hissing" sound as the gas is pumped into the hood. At the conclusion of each session, it takes several minutes to depressurize the chamber. Again, there is some more ear popping and the chamber becomes chilly.

In total, a routine session lasts for 117 minutes with minor inconvenience and discomfort but no pain.

It is hard to get enthusiastic about this therapy. But, think of those who are undergoing treatment for serious burns, amputations, cancer or other conditions. Many of them experience excruciating pain while they undergo treatment. Those involved in hyperbaric treatments should be grateful that their daily visit to a chamber is mostly painless.

Lord, when I start to feel sorry for myself, help me to recall all the people who must pay a painful price for their medical treatments.

A SETBACK

The day arrived for my 18th session. Results so far seemed positive; I had experienced no bleeding since the 5th day. Today was different. I had observed blood and I could feel my bladder retaining fluid. After entering the chamber, I felt increasing distress and advised staff. The "dive" was aborted, the door opened, and I exited the tube. Discomfort became throbbing pain as I was wheeled from the clinic to the hospital emergency room. Waiting for treatment produced new waves of anguish. Deep breathing and relaxation attempts did not help. Finally, a room became available. A group of nurses and an ER doctor quickly worked to make me more comfortable and unblock my plumbing system. Such care leaves you both grateful and aware of your total helplessness and vulnerability. Having others deal with the most private parts of your body is a humbling experience. The staff was kind, respectful, reassuring and compassionate during every moment of my stay. Even more impressive, I was just one of hundreds that received care that day. The service of these medical professionals is a gift to the community.

We are fortunate to have great medical care available. We often take such things for granted; this is a big mistake. First, most of these facilities have been built with private capital that could have been invested in other projects. Second, these facilities are staffed with highly trained, caring and competent people who devote their professional lives to serving other human beings. Third, the facilities are available to all, rich or poor, deserving or not. While the bureaucracy may irritate some, the gentle dispensing of care overwhelms any annoyance caused by hospital, insurance or government requirements.

Father God, make me continuously grateful for the many benefits you shower upon my life each day.

FATIGUE

HBOT is a passive treatment. There is little physical exertion required of the patients. The most strenuous task is to walk up ten stairs to the entrance door of the hyperbaric chamber. Those who use mobility devices don't even have to do that; there is a lift that delivers them to the entrance. Once inside the tube, all are seated on padded benches. It is an overstatement to describe the seats as "comfortable," but they are tolerable for the two-hour session. Some may actually have room to lie down. While treatment is taking place, some will read, others watch videos, and a few may cat-nap. Nothing going on in the chamber can be called work or tiring activity.

And yet, I find myself fatigued at the end of each session and certainly at the end of a week. Why is this, I wonder? The lack of physical activity for an extended period may be a factor. Most of us are used to an active schedule that engages both mind and body. We're on the go from morning to night permitting no time to feel logy. Now we are dealing with 4-5 hours per day of concentrated inactivity. Or, perhaps our ennui is psychological. The implications of our treatment may weigh us down mentally leaving us feeling drained and lacking energy. Whatever the reason, fatigue is a part of this process and must be dealt with.

Fatigue can be an enemy. It is said that most serious mistakes take place when one is tired and not at one's best. We operate most effectively when we feel vigorous, strong and alert. It is important to do your best to avoid those situations that sap your energy and strength.

Lord, please give me the stamina I need to complete this therapy.

UNCERTAINITY OF THE OUTCOME

It would be nice if our bodies contained some type of external gauge that told us what was going on inside. Those being treated with HBOT for such maladies as foot ulcers may be able to visually track the progress of the therapy on the healing of their wound. In my case, measuring progress—if any—is more difficult. From one session to another I do not *feel* different. Do I sense retention of fluid in my bladder? Do I observe blood in my urine? These are the only signals I have.

When I go along for awhile with no negative indicators, I am encouraged and confident that the treatment is working. Then suddenly something happens to jerk me back to reality. I find my optimism was misplaced; I still have a long way to go. Like the old saying, I find myself back at "square one."

In general, life seems to fit this same pattern. We find ourselves working on some project, a relationship or the improvement of some skill. Things seem to be going well—until they aren't. All the effort and activity invested in our activity seems wasted when we are forced to start over from scratch. Discouragement sets in. We may cry out, "What's the use?" This is when we come to the realization that we may not be in control of everything that happens in our life.

ఌఌఌ

What is so irksome about not always being in control? Most people just hate it when control over their life must be ceded to someone else. Lord, help me to understand that your ways are not my ways. Teach me to willingly turn over control of my life to you.

"NEWBIES"

Over the course of 40 treatments, it is inevitable that some of the people participating when you started therapy will complete their course and leave the daily sessions. During this time new people will join the group. It is like riding a streetcar. At each stop, some people get off and others get on.

I remember my first day. I commented about that in an earlier reflection. I was curious about the people I had joined for this therapy. I looked to them for advice about how things worked, asked them questions about the myriad of routine things that take place each day. All were friendly, helpful and willing to lend a hand if needed. That made the beginning stages of this treatment easier for me.

Now I find myself in the role of "veteran" as new folks begin treatment. I wonder if they all feel as I did. Like any random group, I note some of the new people are gregarious, some are reserved. I observe people eager to begin, hoping to achieve a dramatic cure for their ailment. Others seem resigned or distracted, stoically quiet. Perhaps they are dealing with a lot of pain. As in daily life, each person you encounter is unique. I offer advice to those who seek it. I reserve a smile and a few friendly words for those who indicate they prefer to be left alone.

✌✌✌

> *Once again, the hyperbaric chamber mirrors life in the "real world." Some of our encounters with others are momentary, fleeting. Others may be long-lasting or even permanent. If we try to live by the Golden Rule, we are called to treat others just the way we would want them to treat us. Don't you think the world would be a seriously different place if we all followed that principle in our daily lives?*

THE NECESSITY OF HOPE

None of us knows precisely what the future holds. Each person who begins Hyperbaric Oxygen Therapy wishes the outcome of the treatments will be a healed wound, a better quality of life or extended time on this earth. But, none of us received a guarantee about success so we are relying on the virtue of hope.

Author Hal Lindsay once wrote, "A person can live for about 40 days without food, about 3 days without water, about 8 seconds without air...but only an instant without hope." Hope is defined as the feeling of what is desired can be achieved or that events will turn out for the best. Chronic medical conditions can leave anyone feeling hopeless about the possibility of a long-term cure or solution. Many enrolled in HBOT have already faced discouragement about ever seeing a horrific wound healed, the effects of a burn diminished, or tissue damaged by radiation restored. So, all who enter the hyperbaric chamber for the first time bring hope along with themselves.

The human condition means all of us will suffer some pain, anguish or difficulty in our lives. Our human hope may wobble, stagger and, perhaps, come crashing down.

For those who believe in God, there is belief that the Infinite Creator can inject hope into an otherwise hopeless situation. Spiritual or not, we must all find hope somewhere in our souls.

When the doctor told me there was a 70% chance that HBOT would result in a significant improvement in my condition, I was infused with hope. This hope sustains me even during moments of discouragement.

As Pope St. John Paul II wrote, "Never give up on hope...never tire and never be discouraged. Be not afraid." A good mantra for us all.

THE HOOD

A major component of HBOT is the hood. The hood is made of heavy, flexible plastic. It is about 12" in diameter and 24" tall and looks like an elongated hat box. The opening on the bottom of the hood is snap-fitted to rigid plastic collar around the patient's neck and is worn for ninety minutes of each therapy session. The neck ring has two places to connect flexible plastic hoses. One fitting pumps in 100% oxygen while the other expels carbon dioxide. There is an oblong clear face plate on the hood that permits the patient to read or watch videos during therapy.

Once the hood is in place, you notice a faint metallic odor as the oxygen is pumped in. In addition, the plastic smells slightly like packaging materials found on retail products. The most significant impression under the hood is the loud hissing sound of the oxygen being introduced into the enclosed space.

What possible reflection could this plastic device engender? During the course of my therapy, the hood was installed and removed 120 times. It is not the kind of activity I would seek out; I cooperated with the therapy requirements in hope of a successful outcome.

Think of all the things you do each day out of necessity. Commuting to work, completing required but perfunctory reports for your employer, necessary contact with people who don't share your common interests come to mind. Yet, we do these things diligently, honestly and to the best of our ability, not because we like them but because they are part of the fabric of living.

❧❧❧

Lord, teach me the value of doing every task given to me to the best of my ability, and to appreciate each day of life that I have been granted.

GRATITUDE

Those of us scheduled for therapy gather in the waiting room outside the hyperbaric chamber. Small talk often turns to how bad the traffic was getting here today. Someone else may comment that one of the staff doesn't have a clue about how to properly take the blood draw to check diabetic sugar levels. A third person will bemoan the lousy selection of movies or music played in the chamber. Medical transportation companies always get their share of grief from unhappy users. Finally, one person in our group will be criticized for showing up late thus delaying the start of the therapy.

Not all discussion is negative. We often hear lighthearted stories about some amusing incidents that happened last evening or on the way to therapy today. Sometimes a member of the assembled group will share an interesting tidbit about their life or background. We often learn a little about the families of the patients.

I've never heard someone say, "I sure feel fortunate to be here, getting this needed medical help." I suppose many would find this a fatuous statement and not very becoming or "cool." And yet, all of us are taking advantage of millions of dollars worth of sophisticated medical equipment plus a highly trained staff of doctors and technicians while seeking a cure for a medical problem. Perhaps gratitude is the most important mind set we should be bring to our daily therapy sessions.

ৰ৵ৰ৵ৰ৵

We are often blasé about the abundance available to us. How many people around the world share our same medical maladies, but have nowhere to turn for treatment? Continue to remind me, Lord, how fortunate I am to have this HBOT available. Let gratitude be my attitude.

MINDFULNESS AND MEDITATION

Mindfulness is defined as focusing our awareness on the present moment, calmly acknowledging one's feelings, thoughts and sensations. Mindfulness requires concentration on three things: our body; our in-and-out breathing; and our thoughts. *Meditation* is a mental exercise during which an individual enters into an extended state of contemplation about a specific subject.

Both of these mental activities can be very useful inside the hyperbaric chamber. Most of us lead crazy, frenetic lives that leave us little time to just sit and think. Those going through HBOT have a two hour stretch imposed on them each time they are treated. While some will use this time to read, watch videos, listen to music or just sleep, others may gain new insights by practicing *mindfulness* or *meditation*. Even though our minds will often be distracted or drift away, most of us will greatly benefit from trying these two mental exercises.

Face it: We are continuously bombarded with external stimuli from our smart phones, tablets, televisions, radios and the incessant chatter of others. Wouldn't it be great to have a couple of hours each day to think about your situation at this moment, seriously consider dreams you would like to fulfill, ponder the meaning of your life in this vast cosmos or get in touch with the Great Creator dwelling inside of you? Devoting forty sessions to this might actually change your life.

Father Creator, inspire me to use my new-found time inside the hyperbaric chamber to best use. Give me the grace and the will to attempt the practice of mindfulness and meditation.

PATIENCE

Most would agree that patience is in short supply. Everywhere you go, people are trying to improve their position on the freeways, get a better spot in the market checkout lines, or anxious to snag a close parking space. Impatience seems to rule many of life's personal interactions. Some will even agree: "I want what I want, and I want it *right now!*" Rarely do we hear someone say, "Please go ahead of me," or "You first." Impatience is even seen during Hyperbaric Oxygen Therapy.

This is not a blanket rebuke to all in treatment. But, there are little things that can provoke impatience. Who gets their vital signs taken first? Some must wait to use the dressing rooms to change. Someone showed up late and delayed the starting time for the treatment. Why can't I choose my own spot in the chamber? Do we have to watch that movie? The list of little annoyances is long and can affect anyone.

Part of the reason these small issues vex us may be the fact we're cooped up for two hours each day. Almost everyone (except staff) would probably wish to be somewhere else doing things more enjoyable or interesting. The common cry is: "Let's get this show on the road!"

There are times we all need to take a deep breath and just relax. One way or another, we will all complete our thirty, or forty or sixty sessions. The time will pass and we will reach the end of treatment in spite of the little things that annoy us and make us impatient. You can count on it.

≈≈≈

Dear God, I acknowledge that impatience affects me negatively. Help me to understand that my lack of virtue in this regard does nothing to improve my quality of life or interaction with others. Give me patience.

SUPPORT GROUPS

Occasionally you will see in the waiting room a spouse, child or friend who has accompanied a hyperbaric patient. It is obvious that these folks are appreciated and often necessary for transportation or other needed assistance. These helpers become part of the "family" of the rest of us undergoing HBOT therapy.

Any injury, wound or other ailment does not just affect the patient. When a medical condition strikes, people who orbit the life of the patient are also touched. In varying degrees family, loved ones, friends and colleagues may be required to offer emotional, financial, spiritual or psychological support to one in treatment. It can be very difficult for people who need some help but find they have few folks that can, or will, provide support.

Many facing a health crisis or merely a set of treatments are surprised by how many who are willing to step up to help in some way. Family members often represent the "first team" of assistance. But, many of us also have loving and generous friends who will sincerely say to us, "What can I do to be of help to you?" If you have such friends, you are lucky. It is well to remember those who helped you; someday the roles may be reversed, and you will be the one giving, not receiving.

Giving aid is easy. Receiving help is often not so easy. When someone offers to lend a hand, humbly accept. While you may benefit from this transaction, you may unknowingly be helping the giver. Both parties are enriched by any small gesture of assistance.

❦❦❦

Almighty God, help me to be thankful for all who lift me up when I need help. Give me the grace to overcome my natural reluctance to accept assistance when it is offered.

THE LAST DAY

Just another day on the calendar, right? The last day of treatment seemed impossibly far away the first time I stepped into the hyperbaric chamber for treatment. After settling into the routine of going every day, I couldn't believe it would ever end. Like everything else, all things do come to a conclusion; so did this therapy.

What thoughts were present as the hood was removed the last time? I was grateful that this medical intervention was available to me. I represent a tiny fraction of the people who need this therapy but do not have the availability or medical insurance to partake of the treatments. I also felt great hope my medical condition would be significantly improved by having participated. Hope was tempered by the realization that I was never promised a cure. Will it work? As I left the chamber for the fortieth time, I had no idea what to expect in the future.

I thought about all the other patients who shared the chamber with me. Best of luck to them, I thought. May they each receive all the healing they were hoping for when they began the treatments. I also recalled the camaraderie we shared, the courteousness and friendship shown to me over the forty sessions. I made no "best friends", but everyone I met was very nice, had interesting stories, and I enjoyed being with them.

The doctors and all the clinic staff were hard working, courteous, efficient and caring. They did their best for each person in therapy.

Finally, I was grudgingly grateful for the time I had to think and meditate about what this all meant to me and my life yet to come.

Thank you, Lord, for this total experience. Amen.

EPILOGUE

When I contemplated writing this little booklet, I hoped there would not be an epilogue to write. I wanted the story to produce an obvious happy ending where a regime of treatment using latest medical technology produced marvelous and permanent results to my health.

This has not been the case.

Approximately two months after ending the Hyperbaric Oxygen Therapy I find that my symptoms of radiation cystitis have shown no significant improvement. As a matter of fact, a carefully maintained set of records since the end of HBOT shows a worsening condition. I am obviously disappointed with this outcome. I do not consider this a general condemnation of the therapy. I am certain many have, and will, be helped dramatically by these treatments. As a matter of fact, some with whom I shared the hyperbaric chamber have reported to me that they have been significantly helped by the therapy.

Did I waste my time? I don't think so. Given the odds of a good outcome when I started, there was no way to pass up on the opportunity. The unfavorable results were probably a result of my unique medical condition, my body's inability to effectively process the oxygenation and other healing constraints.

So, if this method of medical therapy is recommended to you, give it a serious and hopeful consideration. It may turn out to be perfect for you. I wish you all good luck.

ABOUT THE AUTHOR

Greg Hadley with his wife, Evelyn, lives in Lake Oswego, Oregon in a retirement community. The couple has six children and fourteen grandchildren.

After completing his undergraduate education at the University of San Francisco, finishing his MBA studies at Pepperdine University, and attending the Harvard Business School, Greg spent his professional life in the business world. He worked for IBM and was General Manager of Computer Sciences of Australia. Then, for twenty years, Hadley and his partners acquired, operated and sold industrial companies. Moving from California to Oregon in 1990, Greg established a management consulting practice, spent time as a college educator, author and professional public speaker. Greg continues to assist in civic, political and community volunteer activities.

Mr. and Mrs. Hadley have also been very active members of their parish ministries wherever they have lived and continue with this work even now.

Hadley spent thirty-nine years as an amateur baseball umpire, most at the NCAA Division 1 level. He has authored eleven books prior to this one. See the complete list of Greg's books at the front of this booklet.

Contact him at: greghadley34@msn.com

Breathe Deeply